SAVAGE YARD

SAVAGE YARD

G. F. Harper

LIT CITY

Lit City Publishing
Austin, Texas

Savage Yard. Copyright © 2015 by G. F. Harper.

All rights reserved. First Edition 2015.

No part of this book may be used or reproduced in any manner whatsoever without written permission except in the case of brief quotations embodied in critical articles and reviews.

For information about permissions to reproduce selections from this book, write to Lit City Press at: hello@litcitypress.com.

Books may be purchased in quantity and/or special sales by contacting the publisher, Lit City Press, at: hello@litcitypress.com.

Published by Lit City Press | Lit City Publishing.

Austin, Texas.

Cover by Lit City Publishing.

Art by Leah Katherine Heatley. (Pages: 5, 21, 41, 63, 83, 87)

Email | leahkatherineart@gmail.com

Art by G. F. Harper

Harper, G. F. 1980 –

Savage Yard : Poetry / American / General

ISBN: 0692366202
ISBN-13: 978-0692366202 (Lit City Publishing)

Library of Congress Cataloging Number: 2015902343

Lit City Publishing. Austin, Texas.

Printed in the United States of America.

DEDICATION

My family and friends – I wrote these poems for you. May we live and die a thousand more times.

CONTENTS

Acknowledgments

ONE

007 – fragments
009 – coldness in lament
010 – travail
011 – drunken a.m. preaching
013 – Tom Waits
016 – wrong way
023 – Chuck Taylors, approximately
025 – troubadour
028 – vagabond
030 – girl picking her nose
032 – daybreak sketches
036 – cool breeze
047 – where everybody knows your name
050 – dark things
052 – notes in the margins
055 – consumed
056 – quitting
059 – park bench, Manhattan
069 – wobbly kings
070 – meditations
072 – grasping meaning
075 – trees go by
078 – recall them as they were, as they are
080 – *the idea of America in writing*
089 – sirens
091 – tomorrow
093 – coda
094 – glassy-eyed
097 – camino de la luna
099 – marching along
107 – restless, my soul
108 – bitches brew
110 – workmen, farmers, & the freedom road
111 – awake
113 – blind
115 – I'll be at the table

ABOUT THE AUTHOR

ACKNOWLEDGMENTS

I would like to express my gratitude to the many people who saw me through this book once and again; to all those who provided support, talked things over, read, wrote, offered comments, allowed me to steal their words or recreate their narratives; and to all those who assisted in the editing, proofreading and design.

G. F. Harper

G. F. Harper

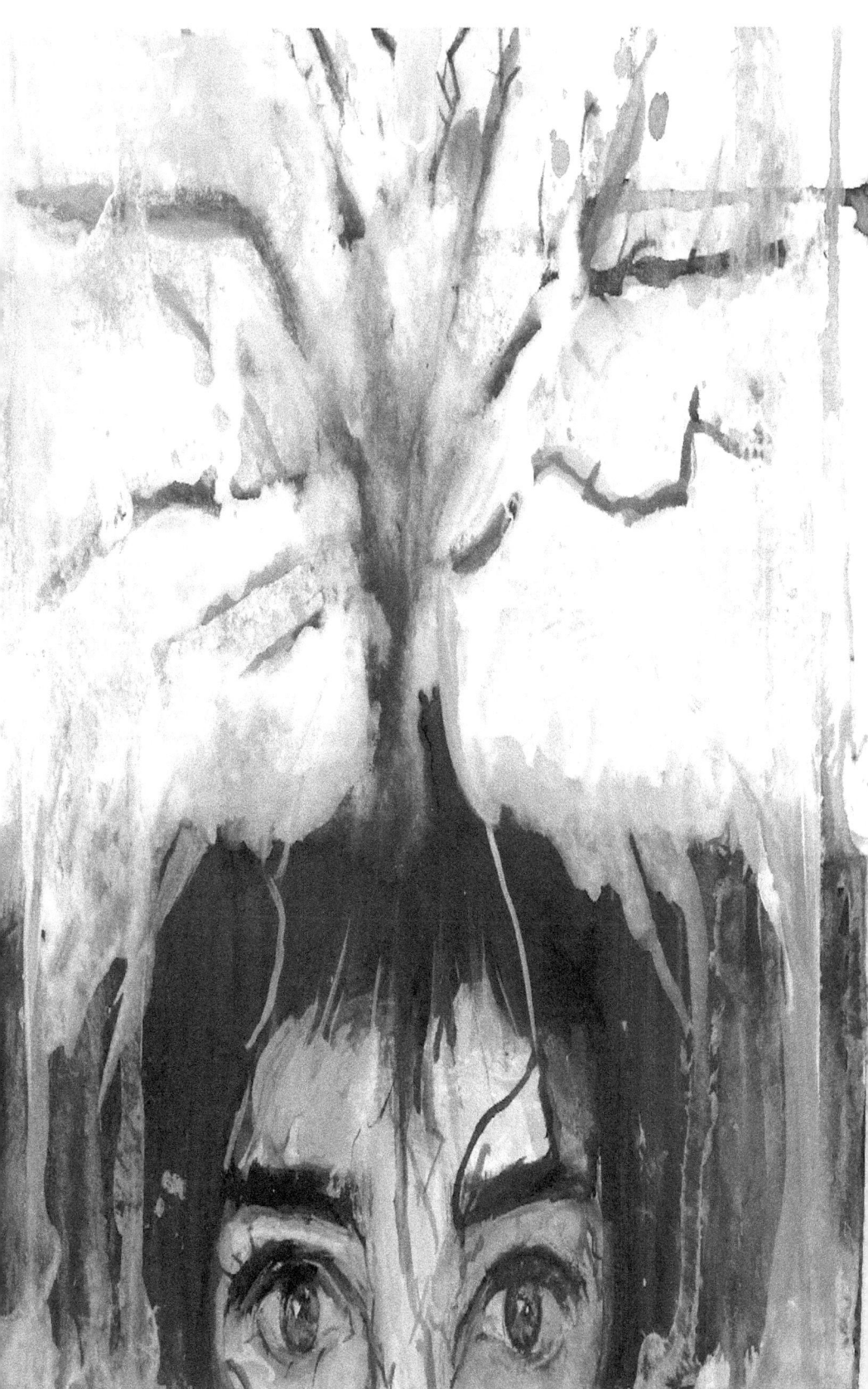

G. F. Harper

fragments

spur-of-the-moment
reflection; abstract gold
burning holes
in your pockets

hard earned cash
spent –
bet you can't buy that
for a dollar though

TV shows
two-bit actor
telling me
where it went

got bad news doc
a heavy load
portrait of a man
suspended, mid air

his legs long, wavy
and bent; another spasm
of existence
swirling madness

renting low budget films
Industrial Revolution
the sensational mid sixties
white noise; some gent

throwing cue cards
all over dirty streets

words too tiny and bold
understanding him

an epiphany
his smirk, my dreams
our wondering
an exercise

of the first amendment
our heart as sound, beats
an incurable rhythm

mass consumption
stealing my soul
living is just killing me

but what a way to go
but what a way to go

coldness in lament

you have shone a brightness
you should have been a map
to carrying on –

all our kinks were caught
iron chained, but not forgotten
an everywhere pain. from here

to here; now there's only shadow
only binds; we broke the chains
once, soon enough we'll rise

pronounced, we'll hear our song
break the stillness; find our voice
mouthful expressions loosed

grackle and crow swelling
becoming giant; rising up

travail

good sunset succor
I believe in your daydream
dawn hides in spent night

drunken a.m. preaching

I raise my hands
in the air, looking
for heaven; didn't find
much, except

the milky dusk
of worn out and
broken
sex symbols

praying for one more
splendor night

one more
nasty piece
of weather

licking at these
red-faced interposed
moments; one more
communion

some days go stumbling
in disappointment; telling
stop resting my body
my faith-desire

in between the bad parts
sometimes I am a dog
searching out alleyways
searching out

whose assignable feet
I should rest my head
at, cunning adulation
I am disappointment

a crop for the killing
I am a dead religion
waiting for bread and meat
waiting for your hunger

put that in your frying pan
sauté it up with a bit of spinach
bell peppers, & onions
the rudeness of friends

and taste a little bit
of God's green earth

Tom Waits

you're alive
a hopeful one
if I could be alive like you
fight like you

trample kick
growl and rasp

if I had steeple curls
upon my head; if I had steeple curls
long sleeve stories
and bye-bye lovers

a neglected angel
flickering at oblivion
two stones
clamoring

if I were the drubbing
hankering fire and fury
always remembering
how emptiness spreads

through the deadness
if I were the fragment

love affairs, weightless expectations
migrating like an old love, half-love
always expecting flames
from the sparks

we are a worn-down dream
on the restless crown
of America; out there
leveraging the lined avenues

you and I in this
strange weather, drowning
us without a vessel; you
and I smile deep inside

slug shell keys play
at the corners
of our mouths
a look half yours

half mine, provoking
the spirit and
vision inside us
spirit of my spirit

you make listeners
disappear into the craving
you make listeners
a radiant eventide

I'm a poem to you
all faces are an unwritten story
to you; impossible sculpting
speech scenes

we are a gallery public
shaping and piecing

a handwritten unmarked song
a long, full moon dragging
into morning; here you come
sewing it all together

all of us, linked bodies
flames from the sparks

wrong way

oh, your sad
tired face
someone said to me once
oh, and if only

I could remember yours
as I sift through

those gone years
hurly-burly across
the days, rearranged
weathered days

coolly in the sun; yours
never on the level
always angled; rapt
bent for someone

not there; deeply foraged
half dead, half alive

Chuck Taylors, approximately

understanding –
looking
for a way
to get rid of

the stains
trying to
dress right
to find feeling

portions of a tune
to every great song

to a place I've never been
oh, shoe soles
full of emptiness
until my shape

my feet
standing
on the sidewalk
9th & Rio Grande

there's always a start
there's always a sorrow

alone, stillness of air
street corner
crossing –
city blues

wave of tree
street light
gathering signals; car honks
foot in a puddle

and one of these days
and one of these days

all the little heaves
all my window thoughts
all this tiny world
fails to drift away

drift away with me
feelings drift away

troubadour

seven blocks
to a bus stop
wet out
somber uncertainty
drunk, sadness
and slumped
young friend
talks of weather –
who talks of weather
American sorrow
speaks of it

a grand and
naked friend
a few weeks ago
mugged

San Marcos
& 7th Street
east of here
he speaks of it

his face,
cuckolded
memory of
everything stolen

even a belt buckle
even his dignity

unbelted jeans
scampering

to his car
keys in hand

didn't take the keys
the sidewalk speaks
of it; downtown littering
speaks of it

disjointed
strangers become
gutters, shoes lament
their consummation

traveled, nothingness
homeless shelter
hundreds odd lives
unnamed

carrying airs
traffic cars, flushed
roaring at days' end
speaks of it

Republic Square Park
seated stranger
passers-by
a minstrel bum
lips like a bard
guitar like a loudhailer
everywhere commotion
speaks of it

soggy seats –
or else stand

rain unfolds; up and down
twenty-seven minutes
till the next bus
stuck

this punchbowl
dance of sparrows and
soggy trees; looking for
a prayer to speak of it

festooned bard sweeter for it

sings his song
Roky Erickson
true love cast out
all evil

the city like a choir

cracked teeth
like a Jackson
Pollock painting
rush-up

of things that break
that fill with somber hues
almost holy
joy walking by

all those carrying faces
glimpses of myself
in them; come and gone
who speak of it

vagabond

Salt-licked hearts
each person sidesteps
shouting anonymously –
cell phone paces

by-passing each other
eschewing struggle
does the pickpocket
still exist; of course

your just desserts –
I feel as a glint might
in the banker's eye

an odd, rolled-up
smear, I am the tipsy
shame dumped
onto the sidewalk

glee isn't a pungent smell
or, happiness is an intoxicating
scented candle

smeared in every suburb
in every upright home

or maybe joy is a rabid
infectious dirge of a dog
impersonating words
alms for the poor

slippery road indeed; I should know
stairwells should know
careful with dawn and
don't dance with strangers

window glass is no cleaner
Ladies and Gentlemen:
are ashamed, yet

I am their sibling
I am their tipping jar

I am the dirt and weeds
so are they, sprigs and hoes
I am the lipstick shade
on his or her lapel

I am chartreuse smudge
myth of happiness

girl picking her nose

I am a last continent
I am a timid in the sails
in a ship; to be learned
discovered —

park benches are anchorage
in the shade of autumn trees

girl picking her nose; bliss of day
fingers can be figurative language

a whisper
of a city

distracted by
its own thoughts

hum tingling
up my spine
maybe, bristled
allergies

wonderful gust
this violet city, its serenade
sweeps; then stays
park trees swell

and break; I clap my knee
to applaud the rustling
symphony; the movement

girl walks on to the beat —

girl without a nose
to pick; girl without
a glance or word; closed mouths
do not drop anchor

we are reluctant boats
huddled against the wind
intercut phones, disconnected

adrift; I am a leaky bucket
pitted against a storm
against consequence

my humanity
pouring out
forever

lackluster days
bliss purple days; trying
for more symphony –
secluded harbors

daybreak sketches

I couldn't think
straight; in a zigzag

way; somehow
on the sidewalk

headlights
carbon feet

a woman
zips by
waves to me

good morning
and vanishes

alleyway
grocery store
sitting down

a long while
to rest my head

a pot of water
little nap before
moving on

to taunt the morning
with my chin high

rain wild rain; gray
and cold; drab sunup

hand in a jar
full of piss

passage of day
busy people

emerging
from a curb

one end to the other
gone as quickly

sonorously
doodling

industrialized
touting the inscriptions

in their throats
coveted like cities

embrace
land-birds

and their lanterns
one end to the other

spit
puddle

of water
freedom

muck

the world
passes by

caves tell stories
shadows

puppets
masters

and the world
passes by

and the world
breathes

and the world
cries

with me
and the world

and the world
soon

will
pass me by

and the world
and the world

lit
by lamp

of people

one end
to the other

and the world
and the world

coveted

monsters
in a cave

cool breeze

Tom sat there
wrinkled butt cheeks
split atop the composite
lid seat

legs pressed against
the cool porcelain
sweat
glazed

tiny droplets drop
merging with
the established sweat
of others

who'd sat there –
and down the drops go
bathing his
Achilles tendon

filled with all that farrago
of fact and fears and
hopes and bacon
cheeseburgers

Twizzlers
bitten into –
a hyena
having a moment

his sweat
their sweat

sinking down
and settling

his skittish twitchy
sphincter whets
in uneasy laughter; anxious
Vitamin D deficiency laughter –

there is nothing worse
than a broken toilet. Except
maybe a working toilet
in a Circle K

Tom thumbs
the malignant pages
of *The Economist*; light fixture
above abuzz

job hunting is a terrific occupation
he thinks of jobs
he thinks of Baudelaire
he thinks of bad-mannered

middle-class economics
Tom is occupied –
he has pressing concerns
slaying him; bills to pay

his America
is an army green
medical orderly
hammering out

pocketknife orders
with the precision
of a 4-year old, neon orange day
crayon dream book

Tom is a dark house
in the evening
gutted fridge
no running water

he would like
to knock on a few doors
to find out why, but
a huge load wages

he sharts
into the basin
of the toilet
ricochet effect

a mess
goddamn it –
toilet paper
wad, wipe

Tom has been living
without a guidebook
he's tied to his mortgage; he's tied
to getting the toilet fixed

he reaches
tugs the lever, flushes
drowns a bit of Eden
the day weeps

pulls his pants up
sweat muddled
now settling –
crevice of his buttocks

perfect islet
of dreams

his underwear
moistened, belt buckle
fastened
an elevator sigh

door knob, smeared –
gust of air,
the whiff gone

to find another
lonely address.

G. F. Harper

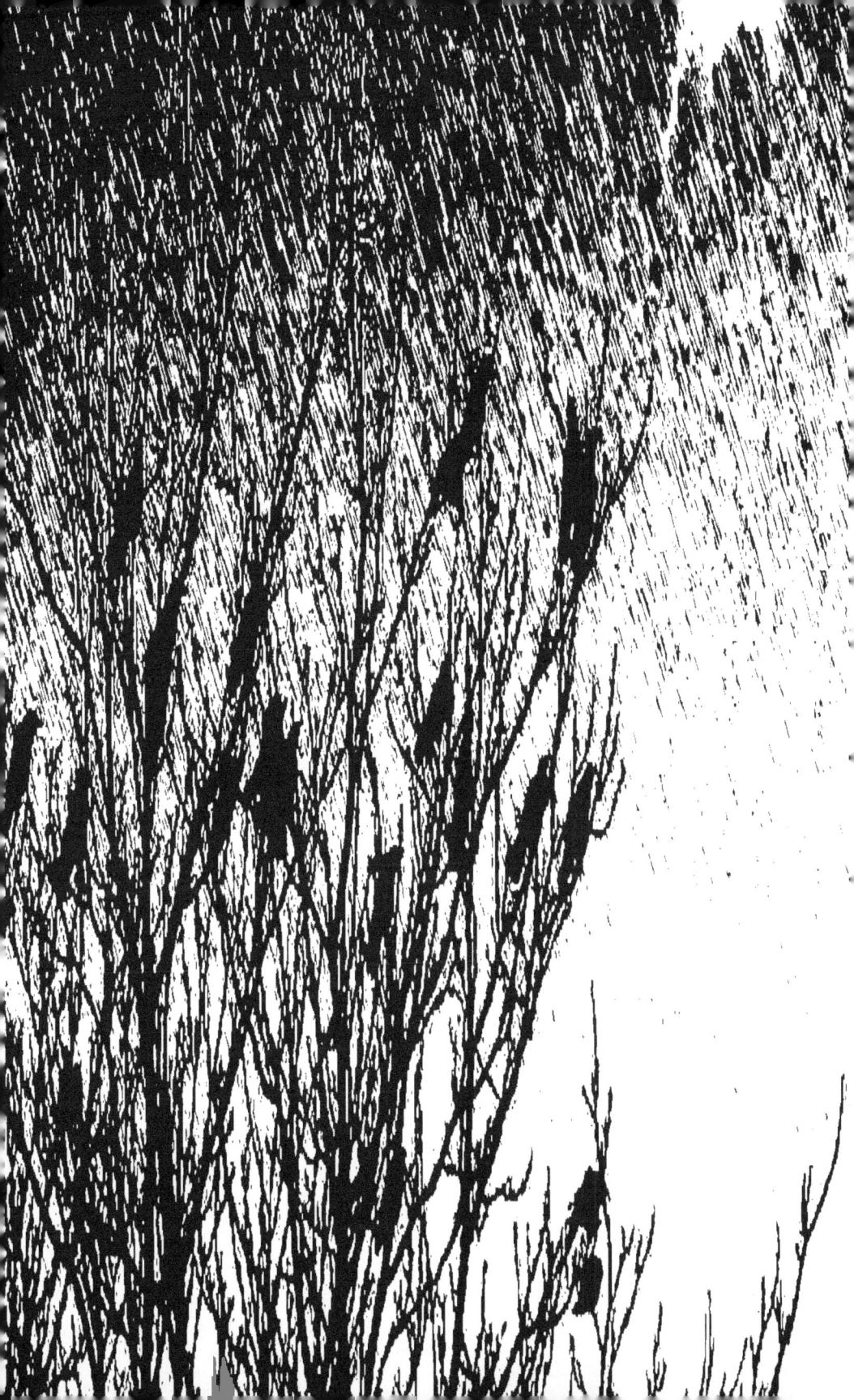

where everybody knows your name

midnight blindness
waking life
set of *Cheers*:

locals
sitting around
barflies notched
in swivel chairs
indented
favorite booths
fermented
drinks between
them

settled
in wait
for old Woody
Boyd

like an inflamed pimple
bursting through
swinging
doors

so they could laugh
just one more good
laugh; but in the back

something different
at work
something
perverse

two strangers
out of place

this bar
this bend sinister,
this fire lake
boiling
in their eyes
seated there

lantern
but dim
Elizabethan gawps
mountainside smiles
dramatist talk
silence

graveyard rites
at the corners
of their lips
cottonmouth
flaked dribble

no stage
nor food,
no drawn and
frothing draft of ale
could quench

the light
dimmed
dark as black
and fine stitched –

Marlowe, you look a bit down.
how've you been?

Is that another one of your attempts at humor?

Shakespeare sits there
namesake
swollen
as a dead
beached
whale

the beauteous
long history of theatre
trapped in a TV box
meshed

into an eighties
theme song hell
over and
over and over

dark things

inside my head
the yea-sayer agrees
all writers
are liars

revealing
the stupidity
the realness
my scavenging

clawing at me

I close my eyes
and see the ugliness
scuttling its way
through

my person –

people are maps
north stars
leading
youth

to old age

human voice
is philosophy
arguing
back and forth

sharing

the world
in our heads
borrowing
from the worlds

of others

my poems
a bad marmalade
from the sphincter
of my heart

plotting

to overthrow
my governing
of this humanity
inside me

these trenches –

well-meaning
melancholy
fissures, break through
spring forth

revealing

notes in the margins

I am a manuscript
a pure river
of coffee and liquor

I am a stink bug
of happiness
and rye whiskey

fortunate breathing –
I am a fat-bellied man
in the early a.m.

touching myself
I am a fly to the stink
emanating

from your words
our flapping screen door
fondness

ripped up arc
of meaning and void –
consumption shop

consuming hope
consuming us
there is no scale

to weigh our failing

to measure
those lost glints

fainter still
there is no prescription
for us; for you and I
young Americans

stars are intimation
at some old world

I am no archetypal
I am no street
I am no earth

I might be the afternoon
when it goes dark; I am
definitely a long stumble –

stumbling toward
your stink, festering

bad poets
are good lovers

fashioned objects
idealistic novelties
like these poems in this book
forgotten

crows
without a nest
lacking a lamplighter
to the enclaves

friendless in a moonless sky –
I don't mind being here

in the doorway
I am a forgotten independence
ingratitude is payment
enough

I like to buzz around
like a fly

honing in
on your unwashed
windows
closed; sealed shut

I'm your broken American
automobile merchandise

I am fascinated
by your greenness
your chartreuse
breathing revs me

your macerated sexuality
geared up

substrate being –
splendor lamplight leather tooled
shadowy street
quality drive

I am yours to break
or to smash, palm first –
poets make good lovers
even the bad ones.

consumed

there's a harvested philosophy
to your exile and poise
Louise Ferdinand Celine –

war is crude, a harsh cry; hunched over
hours to gut rot days, fermented melancholy
pervasions and unkempt notions

that filled you with nauseating dreg
whenever you uncorked yet another pitiable jug
of well-intentioned dark blue merlot

maybe I should learn to hate
as you did, maybe I should learn
to die as you died, maybe

as if there were no other way, as if
time were a dark and tempered room

quitting

it was a matter of
finding other things
to do:
fidgeting

occupying time
ticks; grown
out of hunger
early a.m. gloom

mood swings
cigarette fire, scribing; conferring
in my craw
breathing

tapping
erratic rhythmic
something like –

tap tapping rap tap
tapping; interspersed
palm slap
syncopation crutch

surface thwack
muted cymbal; dulled
sound; scatters
soundlessly

knowingly these are props
desks, tables, countertops

cat on a cool porch
Sunday afternoon
inspiration

sometimes I am the knock
on my head
fingertips:

pen in hand
pencil to temple
rattletrap
on my noddle

addiction is a lone drummer
starving:
for a stage

I was lucky
to have found jogging:
grey distance
becoming

smells; wretched
and flowering
noticeable

all those mouths supping
suckling at the cancer of fate
Elliot claws, scuttling
across the floorboards

narrow, disappearing
my gritty mirror
seeing them

searching
for the face
of everything

my runs, minute
inconsequential
one of many ways

I can teach myself
transformation:

finding substance
in the substrate

park bench, Manhattan

New York City in April —
wheel-rutted streets
full of cars
neither going forward
or backward

day undressing
day pining
stretching
into art into friends
into pubs

Chelsea warehouse district
buildings far-reaching
shade sits
like a backyard
cool and quiet

stretching
full weight of darkness
full weight of light
on the other side —
some of these people

I know; some, I don't
all of us lost in sparks
of shared writing
shared laughter
all of us just enough

to escape the everyday
to light the way out

to find ourselves
on this very street, making
these steps on this sidewalk

I didn't mind a lot of things —
the noise and smoke
the extraordinary buildings
the hidden elements
squalor and homeless dogs

I didn't mind
the upscale forward bundling —
Greenwich is not brimming
any longer
it is carried by the past

paid mind at a city
like a mop and bucket
a city chasing the early dawn
trying to hide something —
I didn't notice it at first

I didn't notice it at first
and then it was hard not to —
conferring with late spring
icy morning; icier still at noon
bum sitting on a park bench

no movement —
his lamp no longer burning
his shoes no longer scribbling
sobering moment
silent before us

life is not a television
nor a shadow brought on by buildings
it either moves forward
or moves backward, ever so
huddled, ever carrying

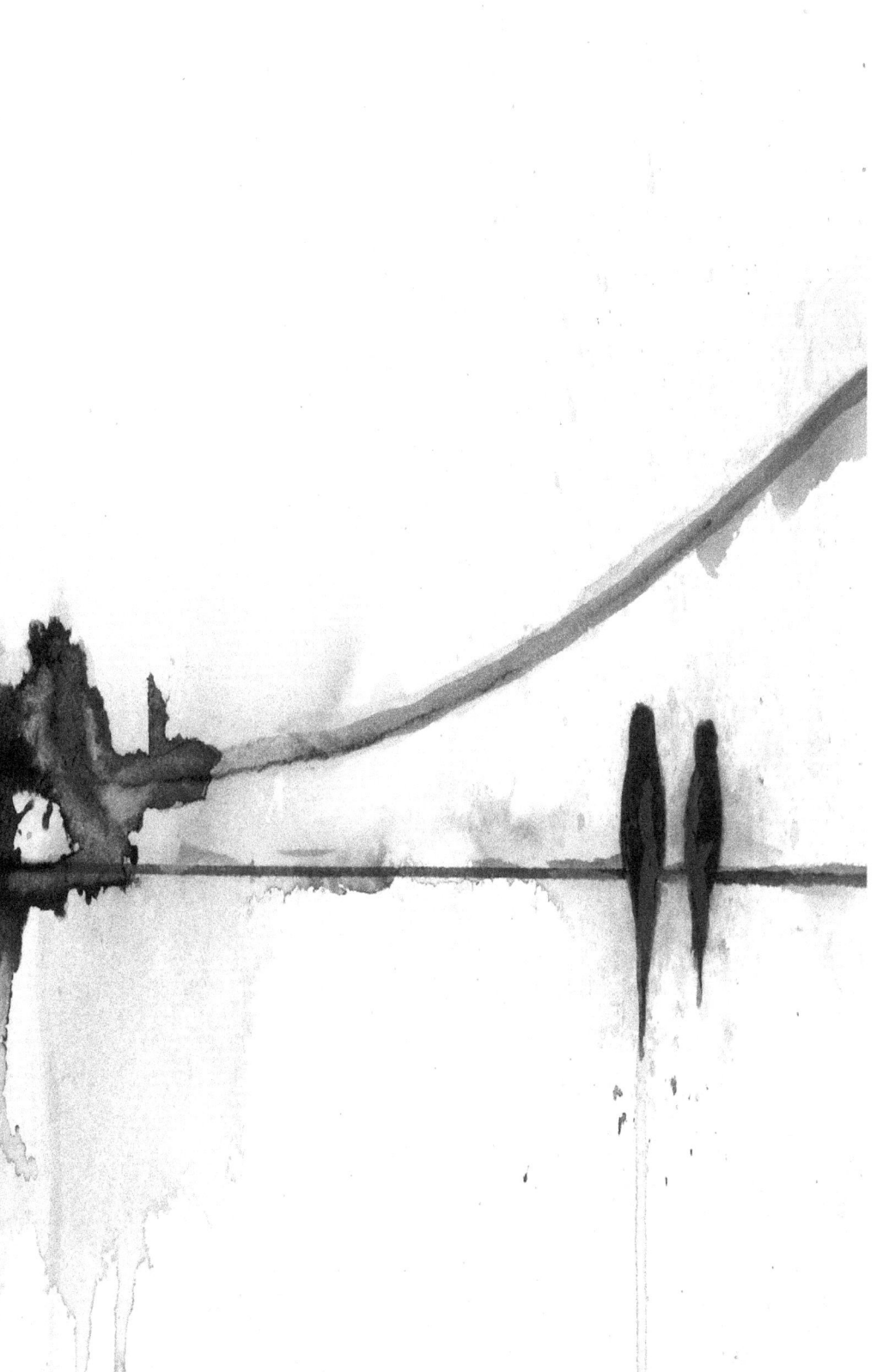

wobbly kings

they got men down in
those man holes – making jungles
out of these tired streets

meditations

when I think
of her tiny face
her tired eyes
harp lineament breathing –
how death met her

led her away
back into the roots
of earth; like rain
falling; like empty footsteps
filling bellyached earth

no answers
just mysterious
undoing; a simple story
like trees grow to wither
to fall; like a mother

loves her daughter
her son; she sees and
knows her children's liberation
from form; from
locked door, opened

from one season
into the next – illness
is a terrible experience
a willowy villain; afflicting
even the darkness

death is a koan
an obvious secret

with nothing to tell
it hides in filled houses
empty houses

it hides behind your eyes
in a 4-year old girl
it hides in her cancer
which ate at her; until
she was gone

death is a sip of coffee
slow-like as if a koan
it is both inadequate and logical
death is a knee
to the groin

but only for the living –
death is a cup in both my hands
an empty chair to sit in
a porch with a view
death is an open-ended koan

to be considered –
I am not death
I am a tree or the tree shade
I am the straw-hat
warmth of the day

marking out my thoughts
my resolve; drifting
cup of coffee; I smile
a skyward reach to the heavens
straightforward day

grasping meaning

I'd like to believe
there's plenty of meaning
in my big toe caught
jammed

deconstructed
badly bruised
in an odd
undoubtedly

avoidable design
unfair jolt. Aye
I say unfair
because I am

wounded with pain
toenail-splintering
pain; however
I am untried

in this
jolt; I've no grasp
of the misery
of my situation

it does not often occur –
the calamity
of a toe stubbing
and until now

I'd never considered
measuring such jams.

Savage Yard

damn these
pocketsize notions
of sense and sensory
how you undo me

gods, give me voice –
voice to explain this absurd
aching situation
this unfortunate trope

once indistinct to me, but
not anymore; ah, fate

fat-bellied swine
you've shown me the farce
that is my foot. once
a blameless lump
hanging there
ten snug and teeny piggy toes
nestled; one, ruining it
for the rest

me; my fool-hearted ways
bare-naked humanity ways
rooted, irate ways
anger, gestures; bloodthirst

yells of obscenities
I grasp; gasp
this bursting-gored-vessel-
cantankerous-throbbing

ah, but nature works
in this; and ah, nature construct
tortures without cause, simple
and little old me

What manner of discourse is this?
What is my toe to be, a story now?
I am no story; plight is not a toe, is it?
should I curse the Gods?

these erected and perverse
designs; always in the way
a coffee table inscribing itself
I was here, I was here

I feel the world's designs
these aches and troubles

I feel aches and troubles
these worldly designs.

trees go by

my dog –
burly companion
name of Louis
Butkus

brown and white coat
the white mostly on the bottom
mighty and observant
American Bulldog

early walks
morning hours
alone; the occasional
stray cat

or early bird
off to work
Butkus trots
neighborhood street

stoic beast
bellowing
from time to time; not a growl
more a yawp; his soul

full of delight
all the trees
all the houses
the smells

passing through him
in a rush, the city

and suburbs mingle
within his lungs

he wags his tail
yawps again and
over the rooftops
it goes

paws stomp
on the graveled streets
as if searching
for more

paws; rough-skinned
singed from the heat
each step reflecting
manifolds of man

onward and outward
his paws full of lightness
scuttling
in little ways

he justifies
his paws
clank clanking, short
and stocky clank

nail-ends scratching
at the surface
searching
the essence

his paws
lettered buttons
his typewriter
collecting

remembering
the difference
between this place
and the next.

even though
we may never fully understand
one another's yawp
I tell his story my way

and he, his stoic knowing
writes another one foreign to me

sun, slowly rising
shaping the sights
back to our house
another day flickers

recall them as they were, as they are

I noticed your book. What's
your opinion on Hemingway?

old man
staring blankly
snaggletooth
grey in the face

mothballs
bouncing
from his ratty tweed
cardigan

I lean in my chair
no exchange of words

drawn out
grinded stretch, calm
like a keen oil well
I look up:

Should we drag this
old horse out?
He banters, he fishes —
raw bait, line cast

his world strong
at the broken places

sigh, coffee
grinding

*I take it you don't like
Hemingway?*

mind reader
more stares
his look begins to loiter
returning to my book

like throwing stones in a pond
he stares and I look up:

*You're a bit of a glutton
for punishment old man.*

You're a bit of an asshole…
he walks away
walks out
the coffee shop

So was Hemingway
I thought

people never listen; and
all good characters, like
people, become
caricatures in life

if you wait around
long enough.

G. F. Harper

the idea of America in writing

all I wanted was Melville
to see me swimming
with his great whale

but, all I can see –

the pale eyes of a desert
girl making small bows, welcoming
the foreigner to her home

I don't want to be a soldier anymore

a mechanism I am not
an alarm clock of fear –
of getting shot at

firing my machine
affirmed trigger
of my M-16

a mechanism
I am not. Sometimes

I feel like a bird –
an albatross

gospel skies, flapping
my yellow-brown-white wings
les fleurs de mal

without cause
only objective

holding tightly to you
America; sometimes

I feel like you're an albatross
a delicate monster; delicate-winged
I'd rather us not fly away –
I'd rather we find harmony

I don't want to be a soldier anymore

G. F. Harper

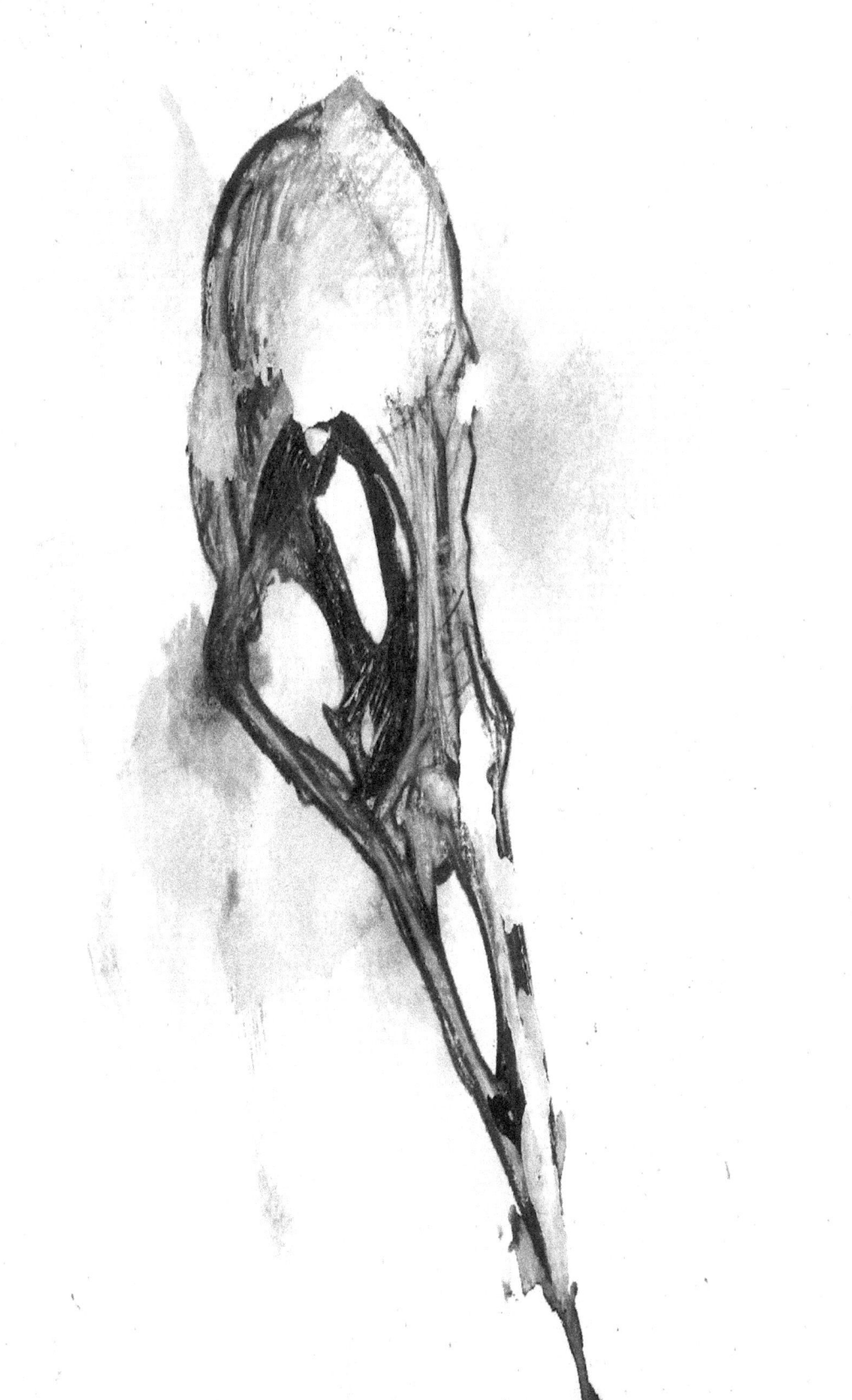

sirens

for as long as I remember
those loud, ascending warnings
have sounded, violently
tragically; distant bugles –

the neighborhood a politic
reality; a farrago of struggle
getting to school without a scratch
my reality; my majestic peace

I didn't mind the gangs
or the drunkards
the unhinged street birds, always singing
always a story to tell

but we were taught to fear
the blue-red-white lights
not by our parents or our siblings
but by them their heavy hammer

and we feared the ambulance –
we thought of them as watchmen of death
it was hard to get along with my stepfather
he was a watchman too

custodians of blood and possibility –
as I grew up
it became apparent
infinitude

this was a reality
in all kinds of places
Chicago, Mississippi
L.A., Tiananmen Square

I was a kid; it was 1989
I can only imagine
the crying, the silencing
empty footsteps

across the ocean
I wonder their stories

their voices muted
by dissonance
burning light
exhausted, spent

tomorrow

don't worry little bird
you'll find a bit of food
forage –
road in, road out
today a parking lot
today a coffee shop porch
today scraps and parts
tomorrow
a ridge of trees
a common battle
an intone of summit
agreeing with the wind

who knows
our little prayers
mine – for my mother
and sisters
my love; my family
who knows yours
perhaps for more leftovers
for more years
more reverie
and humdrum
and humdrum
less obstacle
death and paving

I have an idea –
what you may be thinking
little bird
our culture
is one of madness

it's occurred to me
once or twice too
perhaps I should go foraging
for enlightenment
in parking lots
and coffee shop porches
suffer a ridge of standings
summit
a collective wind
maybe we could conspire
together, little bird

coda

what am I –
if not my dreams
fulfilled

what am I –
if not of the sun

why do we –
only ever feed
our belly
never
our mind

watch
the sunrise
with me –

time
journey
sunset.

glassy-eyed

Matthew— son of
Bob and Sue; heir
to his and her
good fortune

you have their kinky
black curls; your
miserable head
damned as an old poem

or a sloppy human
being, laboring painfully
at trying to make more
meaningful moments

sitting there; arranged for your
class photo; classic snapshot

those eyes of yours, blue
as a notable Russian opus
with an even deeper
cerulean-black

in the pupils; as if
the slow-sugared brooding
was taking note
of what consumed you

in your Sand Dab sickness
flopping around

glassy-eyed fish
out of water; going crazy

from your years drying out
on this earth. You are
no longer looking out
of those poised eyes

of yours; those numerous
dark spots of perversities
and cravings clouding
everything; waiting for death

to come, trapped
in your windowpane; your
addiction, humbling as a God
ever-sinking into the depths

of those morphine dreams
Matthew– sitting there; later on

maybe in class at school; perhaps
imagining the sugar contained
sinking awaiting you in a dark room
in an old grimy-yellowed Victorian

house over on Woodrow
avenue; and in there in that
dark room staring out
at the overgrown, yet dying yarns

of lawn grass; a girl, your junkie
heroine, named Danielle; looking

out her pane, complimenting
oeuvre; waiting for you

to skip class, to come
and muse with her.

camino de la luna

every night I go to sleep
every night as if scripted:
beer in hand
girl on my mind –
the way the sun falls
the way I believe in yesterday
in my friends
in the pigments

of a canvas
in the gun

sculpted words
handwritten liberations
in the blanket gesture
in the workings

of night
and how we draw
from our dreams
in a rapt poem

ah, the dazzle of moonlight
decomposing
blurring life
blurring our trespasses –
I am unimpressed

and I am a sprig of indecision
waiting to take root
someday, someday

my heart will know
the spring beauty

my apartment stairs
won't seem so far up

my sunrise
will have a measure
all its own

marching along

I am no photograph
no tattoo midnight gallivanting
I'm not a sailor waiting
for my boat
to depart
there is no sunset
that is my sunset
I stopped smoking cigarettes
a long while ago
superficial
gazing toward
something
never coming
situational angles
of shadows
and smoke –
every breath unromantic
run down flame
heroine; my savoir
my sidewalk encounter
my breath in dress
letting go
long drawn days
but I've nothing
to let go
I don't need saving
all the sunsets
are my sunsets

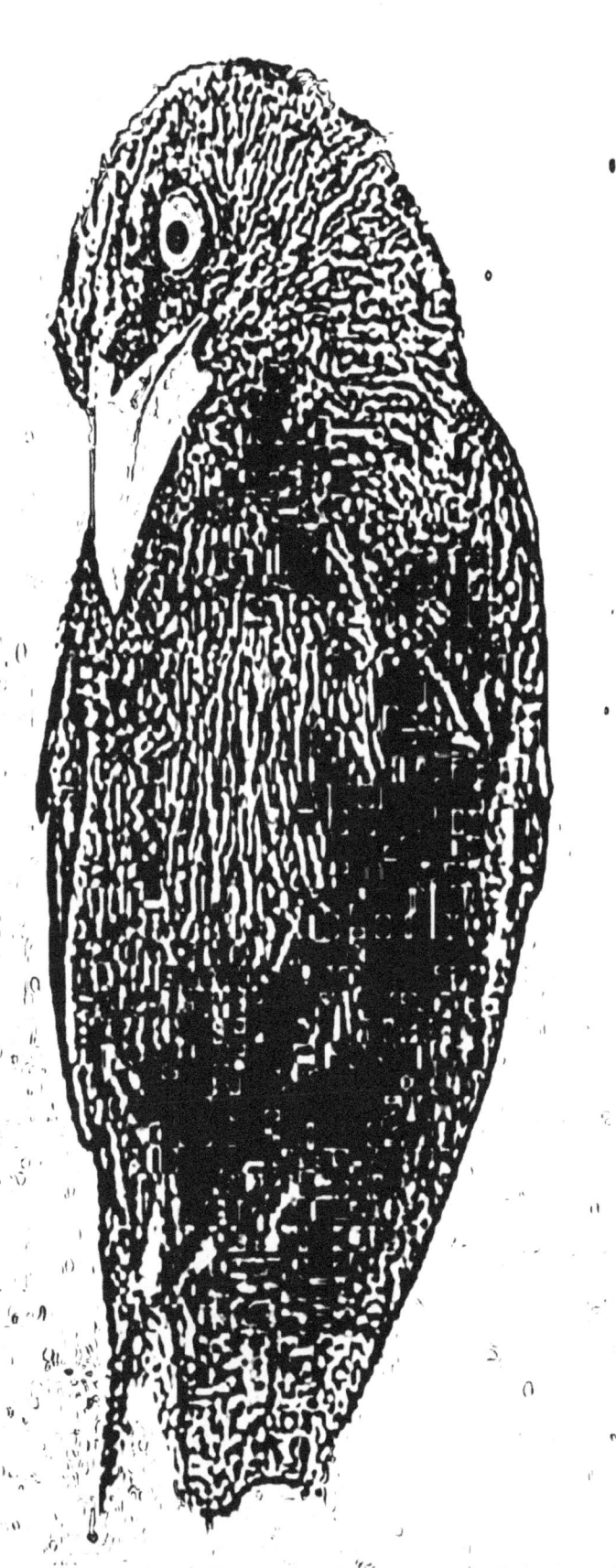

restless, my soul

horizons like to shimmer –
I'm not sure why but
thoughts like this
just creep up on me

I try to imagine
a bird, flying south
for the changing of seasons
its trepidation

ridges are the neck and head
of all that could be different
if the bird could get over; wings
like a fist; brimming forward

bitches brew

string and horns
gnashing teeth
I am Miles Davis
in a story of anger
driving a stolen car
through Thelonious
Monk's dream
I am the chalk images
outlining the street
outlining
the tired weeps
of the slums
I am the opus
context
trumpet
playing
my symphony
of metaphors
humming
little ditties
love and hate
in America
marvelous protests
edible poems
provoking my taste buds
my door has opened
I am the light
of a TV
a smart phone
computer screen
entertaining
reaching

informing
I am holding it all in
that I may embrace you
I am change
without a date, an era
here, and there
I am the gun –
no; never again
I'll never be the gun
anymore

G. F. Harper

workmen, farmers, & the freedom road

growing old in the orchard
my tongue can taste the sweat
on my back
aches rallying against me
arms drenched
it's in the air
too much to voice
long sleeve shirt
over my terrain
child of the sun
crouched
thrashing
my parade is silent
on this imperfect earth
tugging at me
my neck
my trunk perched there
then there; migrating
try to convince myself
I am not a tree to be plucked
uprooted, away
from my family
but I am a human body
deciduous; feed of me
but I am a human body
deciduous; parentage of sweet herbs
scented; feed of me
but I am a human body
deciduous; wild inhabited
knee-bent, measured
the palms of my hands
neither victorious or hungry

awake

I want to be
the impenetrable horizon
creates the day

I want to know
no matter
how wrong I may be
the sky will stay blue
my friends
will still care for me
my family will call

the sweat
shivering
down my spine
is just a march

of gray days
lonely years
absences
mysterious encounters
dear sir, dear madam
I am a strange continuum
a person
of color

my image
in the mirror; image weeping
internal rage; good intentions
I do not have prospects
these days
these days

windshield wipers
don't lift a finger
to help out insects
dear sir, dear madam
foreign and familiar

I'll care for you
I'll be your kite
in an open park
scouting out
the distance
our slumming skyline
seeking out
our immortality

blind

I am a mountain
first, colliding
then, climbing

too busy
with futility-effort
of the universe

I am the ancient earth
receding, road I'll never take
rain erosion

I am a river that laments
pupil – silent partner to my own dying
to this fading

that comes longing
and asks
again and again

if I see like blades of grass
the deeds of man on display
measure of tight-lipped time

ordinary time; her cold body
close, but always moving on
moving faceless shadow

I am the dazzle
of your name inscribed
in the riverbed

and I am at odds
with that which I cannot name –
suspended peaks tugging at me

limestone wonder; I am you
listening like a great basin; caught
in the bellied flood without a boat

I am unimpressed
by all these words
I've seen before

I'll be at the table

I'd like to start building
with my hands
to lean into the smell of wood
cutting through, that weird song
rustling the bones of earth

I want to build something –
a song of leaves and trees
inside a bookshelf
blooming
books like petals

I want to build something –
a weather-worn hem-fir trunk house
inside a family and dogs
not shaped or carved
but cared for

I want to build something –
a constructed pew and box-framed window
into my heart; I want to know people
I want us to grow like a forest
and ponder each other's plights

I want us to be able to come together –
to speak to each other
to understand one another.
I'll be waiting at the table, you
bring the harvest, bitter or sweet

ABOUT THE AUTHOR

G. F. Harper attended Saint Edward's University for a Bachelor of Arts in English Literature with a specialization in Creative Writing, minor in Psychology. Harper also has an Associate of Arts in English from Austin Community College.

Harper currently lives in Austin, Texas.

Savage Yard